THE NAVIGATOR

POEMS

CHRISTIE LEIGH BABIRAD

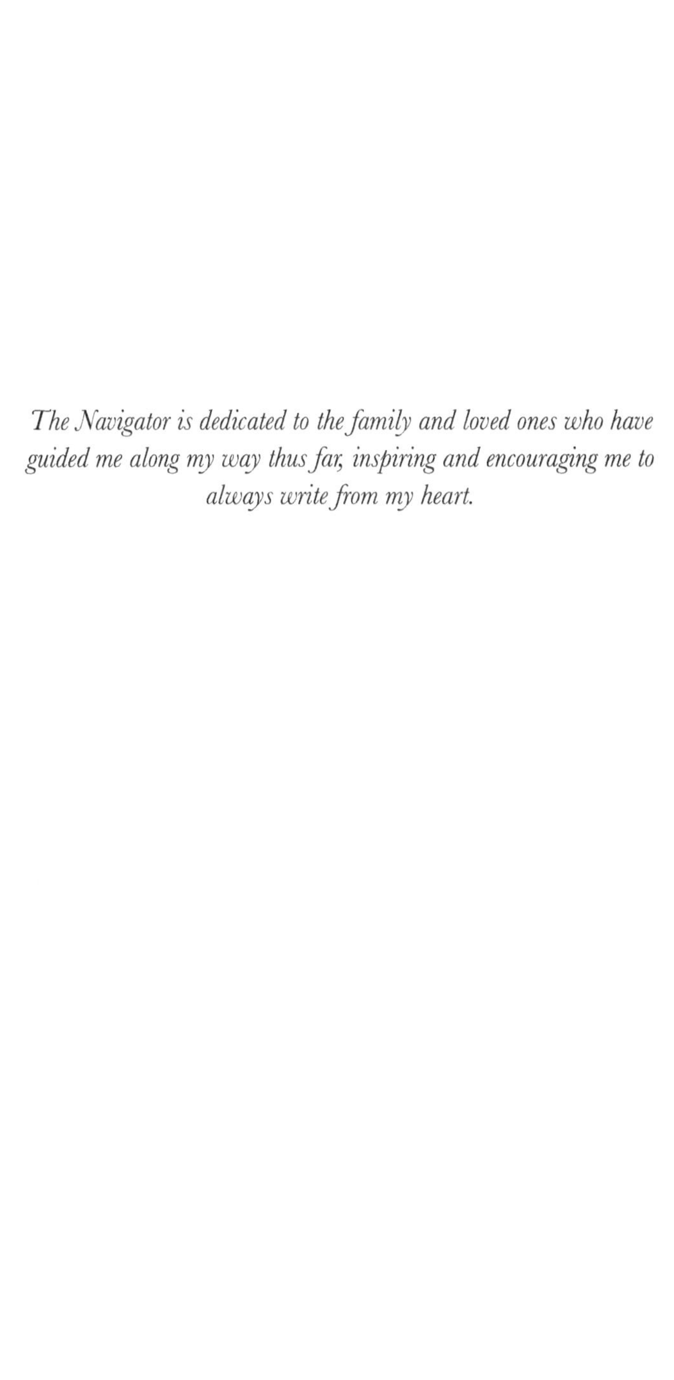

The Navigator is dedicated to the family and loved ones who have guided me along my way thus far, inspiring and encouraging me to always write from my heart.

WHO'S DRIVING?

Down that everyday road,

Brainstorming the next fork to take

As the light stays fixed in the sky above,

A grayish-blue,

And the dashboard clock reads later than we thought.

THE ROAD IS CALLING ME

The road is calling me,

To the on-this-interstate-for-a-while feeling

Of steady movement

Forward.

Blue or gray skies,

A sunrise or sunset painting up above;

It does not matter.

I love getting comfortably lost,

In all the possibilities,

Opening every time I get back to this different kind of home.

I'm thinking it's time,

To get back on the road.

In the Silver Buick

Grandpa's car:

A backseat your legs stuck to on hot summer days,

Black coffee filled the air,

Patsy Cline on the radio,

A couple states over trip,

Time with family was always the job of most importance.

Faith for The Summer

Do you ever feel like you're running out of time?

A golden summer sun blazing in your rearview;

Hearing voices telling you you're too grown for windows down,

Tan legs on the dash,

Music turned up,

That boy looking over at you with light in his eyes,

Believing everything you're experiencing is nothing but true

With nothing but future hope in front of you.

Do you ever feel like you're running out of time—

To be the young and free like you always wanted to be?

Yet, you feel this rumble in your soul that sings the opposite,

A healing melody

Playing out a truth that you're only just beginning,

And not meant to match another's road.

A Summer Road Trip

Setting out beneath the newly risen sun.

Summertime with an early morning chill.

Sweater over a sundress weather.

Drive-thru coffee, the first stop.

Steaming hazelnut flavor filling the air.

Those first few sips, sweet and warming.

Golden light streaming through my hair and across my face.

Anticipation building,

to simply be going somewhere new.

Inspiration flowing,

on this interstate between every forest green mile marker along the way.

Relishing the time seemingly slowed down.

Over three hours before we reach our first destination.

Moving

Moving

Hundreds of miles from home,

Heading to this new place you signed your name multiple times to.

Pitch black sky,

On a highway with few streetlights.

Only a few of you are out here at this hour

With the long-haul truckers.

The dawn feels like it will never come.

Summer night winds stream in through half-opened windows.

Heart-

Racing.

New life-

Rising!

Time

Time will not give you your dreams.

Time will not suddenly sprinkle courage into your heart.

Time will not stop for you to find the perfect place to start.

But time is and has always been

The greatest teacher.

Only a thief when we refuse to fully live,

When we fail to understand

Our dreams come true—

They are the legacy to the world we were always destined to give.

FORMER SELF

She was called Christine.

Afraid to ever speak up,

Wanting to be liked.

To Let You Into My Mind

I wish I could let you into my mind.

The years before you.

What makes me feel the way I do.

And how strong I really am.

Turning crumpled-up paper,

And millions of daylight tears,

Into sapphire stars.

Wanting only to be held for longer than an hour of your time.

The reason why I need to be reassured without having to ask.

And why all I want now is to feel young and alive with you.

I wish I could have you understand,

without me having to tell you,

Why I need what I do from you.

Fiery Soul

Born under fire

She lights with pursued passions,

A relentless heart.

Why Only A Fairytale

Why does love have to stay a fairytale?

Why can't we have what the stories relay?

Why do we have to ruin it all?

All I want is a strong man,

Soft but passionate,

Someone who knows what he wants,

And does not waver in his interest

No matter how many other beautiful ladies are at the ball.

He knows what he has with me,

And he values me and loves me deeply.

Little Girl

Little girl,

taught to rationalize her hurt.

Think deeply about everyone else,

but do not dwell on oneself.

Little girl,

always be a lady.

Keep your hands folded in your lap.

Listen more than speak.

Little girl,

do not ask for anything from anyone.

Keep your tears to yourself.

Be outwardly soft, but inwardly strong.

Hi, little girl, it's me,

it's you, twenty-seven years from now.

I want you to know that you are wonderful just as you are.

Little girl,

all you need to do is always be true to yourself,

and you will never go wrong.

No matter what mistakes you make, as we all do, along the way,

little girl,

you will be fine as long as you remain loyal to all the beauty that lives inside of you.

TEARING DOWN

Do you ever feel like burning every bridge

To see if anything real remains?

Do you ever feel like you no longer care to care

When too many times there is no hand reaching out for yours?

Do you ever feel like it's time to STOP?

Stop pushing,

Stop desiring,

Stop twisting,

Just STOP.

And FEEL

The blank slate emptiness you've been trying to deny.

Do you ever want to just burn down every bridge?

In the Middle With Him

No one is worth sacrificing your joy.

But what happens when your joy,

Sweeter than ever before,

Has been found in your time spent with him?

And you are tired.

You are so tired of having to work so hard,

To dig up all that is within but will never equal the same kind of love.

Yet still,

What do you do when what is given is the minimum of what you long for,

Just enough to keep your heart beating with his?

A Gemini Kind of Town

I live in a Gemini kind of town,

Supposed to match my fire flame,

But sometimes these opposites don't attract.

You soften me by the ocean.

Your sunsets kiss me just right.

You've got me certain you're the place for me.

Your city lights stir my imagination,

Intoxicating me with romantic visions,

You get me dreaming my young wishes can still come true.

But then winter and spring strike my heart heavy.

Belle's storybook village becomes you.

All too many of the people appear Gaston-like.

The cold is bitter and the sun shines too bright.

But this Gemini town has got me tied to my roots.

And I wouldn't trade this upbringing for anything.

This place has made me passionate and strong,

Has me fighting when harsh realities come,

Knowing that like a Gemini, I can move with the ever-changing tides—

Always remaining determined and true to who I am deep inside.

THE TRUTH ABOUT SPRING

Spring

Bright, Quick

Blooms, Transforms, Changes

Uneasy, Emotional, Renewing

Growth

Soul Sharing

Did I share my songs with the right man?

Those melodies I thought could belong to us—

I was pulled,

Fervently,

To have you listen

And hear

What I heard,

Feel,

What I felt,

With lyrics that fit our memories,

Like the songs were written specifically for us,

For the way I feel about you,

The way I hope you feel about me, too.

Checking Off The Day

I'm checking off the day.

I have no more to say.

I'm keeping that hurt over humans' inconsiderateness at bay,

This is not something to other hearts I choose to relay.

I want the hope of tomorrow to stay,

The belief that this next day will shine a greater soul-awakening ray.

PRESENT DAY

We don't get along anymore.

Topics always turn.

Conversations are stilted.

And separation is now peace.

I miss the way we used to be—

Together,

listening to the music we shared,

driving from darkness to dawn,

both holding the knowledge that we would find our way.

No "More"

I don't believe it is MORE I crave.

It is LESS that I desire.

LESS doubt.

LESS ache.

LESS wondering which way you will turn.

CONFIGURED

Like a flower leans to the sunlight;

I hold hope,

Hide hurt,

Light love,

Twist turmoil

And believe in a righteous reason,

A delicious, destined destination.

Torn

He says you need to have a thick skin,

but I plead for understanding

that he cannot connect to—

how this feels,

to still have open wounds,

bad blood and toxic air still flowing through,

and yet I still keep pushing on,

moving beyond the pain,

pretending it does not matter to me at all;

Keeping palms pressed to the closed door of all my sensitivities—

I make sure this door stays shut and the room stays quiet.

It's all so exhausting

When all I want to do is fall into what comes naturally—

my softness and heart,

only desiring to be loved,

and heal the world through the pain I have experienced
and witnessed.

Simple

I only wanted you to want me.

I only wanted you to claim me,

Say this is "My Girl"

And for this to feel good and true to you.

I only wanted you.

I only wanted to claim you.

You had me saying this is "My Guy"

And I have to tell you—

This felt good,

I felt that these words I spoke were true.

Heart-Struck

I think about you

When the wind stirs the branches and leaves,

After days of bright sun and stillness.

I think about you

And wonder

If today is the day

You will recognize how deep my heart is for you,

You committing with desire

To not take this love for granted anymore,

That you will be heart-struck.

Quest for Control

Chasing—

the job,

steady footing,

alignment,

experiences one ought to have,

all the while in discomfort,

knowing, what is most worthwhile,

and meant to be part of my story,

cannot be chased.

Who Says?

Who says the order things have to be—

If he didn't bring me roses at the start, he never will?

Who says the time love takes—

If "I love you" comes first to one before the other?

Who says I can't say *Come Back*

After an in-the-moment-certain goodbye?

Who are these people saying so much—

Like any of us have any clue once the heart is involved.

And what is the point of this life if you aren't living within your heart?

Who can truly understand these snowfall-of-feelings inside of me,

Feelings that have me feeling so completely alive

And say,

This is wrong?

The Navigator

The Navigator is both me and you.

No matter how passive a personality can be,

There are a multitude of moments when each of us must take the helm.

Unsure hands at first on the wheel.

At times we feel well-suited and capable in our role.

Other times, the storms and variables seem impenetrable.

Every time, though, when we are the captain we add color and definition to who we are,

And the person we are continually becoming.

LATENT

Her confidence.

Her potential.

Every single one of her dreams.

If only she could get comfortable underwater to see,

The full, dripping off the pallet,

Easter bright colors she possesses.

Spinning Through Time

Aren't we all,

Spinning

Through time?

Sometimes I feel that I am

Spinning,

Too fast,

Through moments

I'll wish I could have held onto,

If only this was possible.

And so I try better next time,

To savor more each time,

The moments as they come,

To remind myself of how lucky I am.

Replaying,

Reflecting,

Upon my memories,

The moments that have not faded,

That still swirl,

Round and round in my heart.

Control

Control—

A hazard to herself,

Often leads the ship to greater turbulent waters.

Unnecessary

Stress

And fear,

She misses out on the stunning sunset,

The single dolphin everyone else is still reeling from spotting,

Awe in their retelling.

Control misses all of this.

Always wandering.

Always seeking.

Always on edge.

I strive daily to move further and further away from her pull.

PERSONALITY TYPE

She took the interrogation in

And gave you society-approved responses.

She smiled to counteract your judgment.

And she had you believing—

She valued the questions you posed,

That it was perfectly reasonable

To try and get to the bottom of another human being this way.

You were secretly hoping the cracks would be revealed to you

Right then and there.

But she has met your kind multiple times before.

How frustrating.

Not For The Tender-Hearted

This full human experience is not for the tender-hearted.

There needs to be a strong will,

When you lay your head down and you are—

Flooded

With emotions of misplacement,

And realities—

Oh, how ludicrous this life can be

Enveloping every inch of you.

When you are devastatingly awakened,

Like a thunderbolt to the chest.

And you ache—

For all the loved ones you miss,

Snatched away by fate without any concern of goodbyes.

Yet, you still long—

To put your soul out there,

To see more,

Feel more,

Be more.

A Big Problem

There are so many souls

Floating.

They don't know who they are,

What they love,

What they stand for

But,

They spout their momentary convictions onto others.

They don't take the time to listen,

To step outside themselves and their own experience,

To offer up pure love,

An unspoken understanding—

We know very little in this ever-changing world

But,

To be kind.

These souls sadly cause the most widespread heartbreak,

A war of other's opinions that some souls spend years trying to recover from,

And some are unfortunately unable to rise above these toxic stances.

These Pictures

When you view the highlight reel of your peers,

Do these pictures make you feel a certain way?

But this is like looking at a perfectly landscaped house from the curb—

You have no idea what goes on inside the walls.

You don't see the sacrifices,

experiences,

heartbreaks,

and unique paths the residents must navigate through—

tales inevitably filled with wonder,

but also,

a lot of grit that no one would want to reveal to the outside,

just like you.

As the Situation Stands

Breaks her heart

To stay away,

To not answer,

All to love you.

For these dragons,

They can't be slayed by anyone but you.

The things you say,

The swords you toss without a thought,

Cut deeply.

But she'll be okay,

As long as you're okay.

Transformation

Steady this dusty heart,

Wrought with conflict of change,

And time ticking too fast.

The Test

Today was a tangled Christmas lights kind of day,

Where moments of clarity refused to stay.

Anxiety over a choice of movement was not kept at bay.

Passing the day's test of character would be the pay,

For the forming of a diamond is in the pressure, the wise say.

To Live with Spirits

How do you navigate the death of an exquisitely lived but cut-short life?

When you can't turn the compass in any direction without feeling a lack of acceptance.

Because you can still see them walking into your house.

You can still hear their voice.

You can still feel the warmth of their embrace;

The sound of their joyful laughter,

you can't erase.

Not that you would ever want to live without their presence.

But how do you exist knowing you can't reach them the same?

The need remains because you can still feel their heart beating with yours.

I can only conclude the answer is to hold tight to the being you love so,

The presence you can wholeheartedly still feel.

You need to allow them to breathe into you,

To accept

They must not truly be gone,

That no one in reality truly dies.

Who I Look for Now

I'm looking for the souls I can tell my dreams to,

With the excitement of a child,

Because that's the only way to be with dreams.

I'm looking for the mates who will join me,

Finding the uncovering of these buried dreams as fascinating as I,

Stirred to tap into their treasure chests as well.

Sparked together.

I'm looking for my collaborators of joy,

People who echo the beliefs I hold tightly to,

That this is a big, beautiful world,

Open to us all,

No matter the hitches that lie on our individual paths.

Take Me To The Water

At the water's edge

I release expectations,

Feet grounded in sand.

View from the Bridge

The ocean is choppy,

White-capped waves as far as the eyes can see.

The ferry's engine roars with safety measures for the impending storm.

And I stand alone, on the boat's bridge,

The summer wind whipping through my hair,

Strands tangling and sprayed with the moisture in the air.

And I calmly gaze out at the water and great big gray-blue sky,

My heart as wild as the day,

My thoughts consumed by desire,

To break apart from all that is not solid in my world.

CALL TO THE OUTSIDE WORLD

I've got to get out of this rut.

I've got to get out of this sunken feeling.

The people say you need to be content alone.

The people say you need to love yourself before anyone else can love you back.

But what happens when you've been there, done all of that?

When you're exhausted from every bit of motivation coming from within.

When you've made friends with all your ghosts,

And accepted everything there is to accept.

When you simply want a small piece of society to say to you—

"Yes."

"I like what you're doing."

"Keep going."

"I am with you."

Running My Heart Out

I'm running my heart out

Past

The dirt garden a few weeks ago was pink roses.

Poetic, don't you think?

I'm running out the memory of you

Singing to me

"Brown-eyed girl,"

The association of my lake to you now—

All because of the many thinking-of-you photos I sent you.

I'm running out the memories

Of your gaze—

Anxious,

Excited,

Wanting no one but me,

Or so I thought.

I'm running out the overwhelming hurt,

The bitter sting that will tighten my heart—

I don't want that to happen.

I'm running out this hollowness in my chest

That makes me

Fight

For my legs to keep pushing forward,

To keep breathing—

In and out,

To not give up on the belief I had before you.

I'm running my heart out

To clear my soul

For the hope of tomorrow.

Love is A Garden

Love is a garden.

You may have heard this before.

If the love is true,

All of the land must be tended to.

If attention is solely given to the lush red roses,

Allowing all the other flowers to wilt,

The garden in its entirety will not grow

And the roses will lose their appeal.

Like the most precious attributes in the one you adore,

There needs to be attention given

To every part of her,

Every part of him.

The little moments,

The subtle nuances,

You need to water daily

If your love,

Like any living thing,

Is to flourish and grow.

Love's Disappearance

You will not hear from me.

I am moving blind

Through the ache,

Past my instincts,

Beyond my heart,

Undermining what my soul needs

All for the time being.

To give you the room I know you need.

To love you the only way I can.

To believe.

To have true faith

You will see,

You will feel

How great my love is for you,

Stretching higher than the tallest, steepest mountain climb;

Holding space,

Staying open;

Hopeful for your eventual call.

Consider the Source

One of the best pieces of advice she has ever received,

To *Consider the Source*.

When an individual's actions, judgments, and advice

Contradict everything you believe—

Take a breath,

A moment of peace,

And peer into who that individual truthfully is to you and others, as you see.

And then ask yourself,

Should they have any power over you to shift what you honestly feel?

I think not.

Keeping the Door Open

They say he ain't gonna change,

He told you where he stood.

You might think you love him,

But this will never be love.

She hears them,

Understands the side of the river they are on,

But she's not looking to change him.

And she's not the wavering kind,

The forgetting the sparkling, glittering stone kind—

The one you picked up and kept as a child,

The one she saw in him.

She's growing in wisdom, heart, and experience every day,

And that is the hope she sees in him—

Every day a little less fearful,

A little more of wanting something great—

A little less self-orchestrating,

And a little more open to the river's flow and path—

The same as she.

Something to Maintain

Staying true

Can be difficult

With changes

and fresh storms,

but is a reward to achieve,

a place of return.

Silencing the Chatter

I'm going to be right about you,

My slow burn,

Winding path

Of subtly sweet signs

In a forest of expectations,

And state placed markers I'm weary of seeing anyway.

I'm tired of the following.

I have heard the end game stories of the rule book readers,

The deal-breaker touters;

And I must say,

My heart holds onto you

The same as the blood that travels through my veins.

I know you are right for me,

No matter how the trails and route may change.

Love Spell

A spell of love,

Yes, that must be what I am under.

Pine cologne,

The scent,

Floating in on fluffy clouds,

All around me.

Making moves to the sunshine,

But my hand is guided

By a sweet Prosecco going down feeling,

To the intoxicating,

Grassy and crisp aroma,

The atmosphere that is you.

Turning toward a nightfall summer rain,

And candlelight

That lights the way,

Forever into you.

Attached

She likes the way you hold her hand,

the way you move your fingers across her skin.

Your touch remains

long after you leave.

And her soul no longer feels entirely as one.

Do You Want to Know?

Do you want to know

How I ache for your arms to be around me

in the middle of the day,

late at night?

There's no telling when I will be struck with thoughts of you

All around me,

my mind,

my heart.

When you listen to me the way you do,

Your curious "tell me eyes" looking directly into mine,

How your hands welcome me into your body

so smooth.

Do you want to know—

How you make me feel

Like the most beautiful pink rose,

delicate with you,

cherished,

and wanted beyond any other being?

Rainbows

She seeks rainbows now,

To water belief in her—

Miracles remain.

Embracing the Wind

I'm embracing the wind

that reminds me my heavy heart is strong.

I'm embracing the wind

that sings of positive change.

I'm embracing the wind

that teaches me it is good to shake up one's life every once in a while.

LED BY SERENDIPITY

When we set out on new adventures,

We don't fully know what we will be navigating,

No matter how meticulous we plan.

I set out to uncover my past,

And the present came on me like radiant and at times wild summer waves.

I thought I would be crossing paths with different versions of myself,

And I uncovered my steady identity with each step I made.

I planned on going on this voyage alone,

And I found love,

The kind that extends the trip,

The kind that makes the journey more than I could have ever imagined.

Acknowledgments

Thank you to my family- Mom, Dad, Robbie, and my sweet Jack Russell-Alistair. I would like to thank Harbor Lane Books for believing in my poetry- the genre of writing I enjoy the most of all. Thank you to all my loved ones, here and in Heaven now, who have been so very supportive of me and my work. And lastly, thank you to all my readers; it is my hope that my writing connects with all of you and enters your heart in perfect timing and in just the way that it needs to.

About the Author

Christie Leigh Babirad is an award-winning author and poetess of 7 books in total thus far. Her work has been featured in *Bella Grace Magazine*, *Dan's Papers*, *The Babylon Beacon*, *Amityville Record*, *Massapequa Post*, *Tiny Buddha* and *The Mindful Word*. The primary hope she has for her readers is that her words and stories comfort and inspire. All her books are available via Amazon, B&N, and through other major retailers.

Facebook @authorchristieleighbabirad

Goodreads @cbabiradauthor

Instagram and Pinterest @christieleighbabiradauthor

About the Publisher

Harbor Lane Books, LLC is a US-based independent digital publisher of commercial fiction, non-fiction, and poetry.

Connect with Harbor Lane Books on their website www.harborlanebooks.com, TikTok, Instagram, Facebook, Twitter, and Pinterest @harborlanebooks.